THE TRANSCONTINENTAL RAILROAD

Turning Points in American History

THE TRANSCONTINENTAL RAILROAD

Marilyn Miller

Silver Burdett Company, Morristown, New Jersey

Cincinnati; Glenview, Ill.; San Carlos, Calif.;
Dallas; Atlanta; Agincourt, Ontario

Acknowledgments

We would like to thank the following people for reviewing the manuscript and for their guidance and helpful suggestions: David Williams, Professor of History, California State University—Santa Cruz; Katherine Allen, Librarian, Chatham Borough High School, Chatham, New Jersey.

Front Cover: Library of Congress
Back cover: "Driving of the Last Spike" by Thomas Hill courtesy of the California State Railroad Museum
Title page: Library of Congress
Contents page: Library of Congress

Library of Congress Cataloging-in-Publication Data

Miller, Marilyn, 1925–
    The Transcontinental railroad.

    (Turning points in American history)
    Bibliography: p.
    Includes index.
    Summary: Describes the construction of the Central Pacific, Union Pacific, and other related railroads which joined the east and west coasts by meeting at Promontory Point, Utah, and views both the early days of railroads preceding that event and the effects of the transcontinental railroad thus formed.
    1. Pacific railroads—Juvenile literature.
[1. Pacific railroads. 2. Railroads—History] I. Title. II. Series
TF25.P23M55 1986   385'.0979   85-40167
ISBN 0-382-06824-6

 Created by Media Projects Incorporated

Series design by Bruce Glassman
Ellen Coffey, Project Editor
Charlotte McGuinn Freeman, Photo Research Editor, Editorial Associate
Michael A. Wong, Editorial Assistant
Bernard Schleifer, Design Consultant

Published simultaneously in Canada by GLC/Silver Burdett Publishers.

Manufactured in the United States of America.

CONTENTS

INTRODUCTION

THREE DOTS FROM PROMONTORY POINT

On May 10, 1869, it was clear that something big was happening in the small, ramshackle town of Promontory Point, Utah. Two splendid, shining railroad trains stood one on either side of a one-rail gap in the track, separated by a large crowd. The train on the western track was headed by the Central Pacific Railroad's Jupiter engine; on the eastern track the train was headed by the Union Pacific Railroad's Engine Number 119.

Early in the day, officials of the railroads, and their guests, had descended from the elegant private cars behind the engines and mingled with the crowd. An army detachment cleared a space in the crowd so that the guests and speakers could make their way to the appointed site. A band began to play as a Chinese construction crew from the Central Pacific

May 10, 1869. The Union Pacific's Engine No. 119 (right) and the Central Pacific's Jupiter (left) meet at Promontory Point, Utah.

and an Irish crew from the Union Pacific laid down the last connecting rails.

In the midst of the commotion, the telegraph operator, seated at a table next to the track, tapped out a message to be received in Omaha, Nebraska: "All ready now. The spike will soon be driven. The signal will be three dots for the commencement of the blows."

All across the nation people awaited those three dots. Parades waited to start. People stood ready to ring church bells, to unfurl flags, to fire cannons.

Back in Promontory Point, a silver hammer was raised by Leland Stanford, the governor of California and one of the four heads of the Central Pacific Railroad. The crowd grew silent. Governor Stanford was to drive in the last spike, joining the two railroad lines that had been under construction for so long. He was to be joined in the task by Dr. Thomas Durant, the vice president of the Union Pacific.

Leland Stanford, one of the founders of the Central Pacific Railroad, later elected Governor of the new state of California

Thomas C. Durant, Vice President and acting Chief Officer of the Union Pacific Railroad

With their two blows, the railroads stretching from the east and west coasts of the country would be joined for the first time.

The two railroad companies had been racing against each other since 1863 to see which line would lay more track and reach the meeting point first. The Central Pacific had been building eastward from Sacramento, California, while the Union Pacific had started its drive west from the plains of Nebraska. The federal government had decreed that the two railroads were to link up at Promontory Point.

Governor Leland Stanford swung the silver hammer at a golden spike, which had been fashioned especially for the occasion. A roar of laughter broke the silence; Stan-

ford had missed. Dr. Durant took the silver hammer. He, too, swung and missed. The excited telegraph operator tapped his three dots anyway, moments before the Union Pacific's chief engineer finally drove in the golden spike. The Union Pacific's Engine Number 119 and the Central Pacific's Jupiter gently touched, signifying that the entire railroad line had been traversed. The engineers of the trains each broke a bottle of champagne over the other's engine and the dignitaries shook hands all around. After a series of celebratory speeches, an elaborate lunch was served for the dignitaries in Governor Stanford's private car on the Central Pacific's Jupiter train. Outside, the crowd feasted on buffalo humps and celebrated with whiskey, all provided by the Central Pacific.

As dusk fell, the two special trains backed away from one another. The Jupiter was to return to San Francisco and the Number 119 to New York. That night, Promontory Point was the scene of a torchlight parade, a banquet, and a grand ball.

One person in the nation did not celebrate. In Greenfield, Massachusetts, the widow of Theodore Judah locked her door and refused to see any callers. Later, she wrote about her feelings on that day: "It seemed to me, as though the spirit of my brave husband descended upon me, and together we were there [at Promontory Point] unseen, unheard...."

1

THE ROAD TO PROMONTORY POINT

Had it not been for Theodore Judah, there might never have been a race to Promontory Point. The road to Promontory Point, however, began not in the United States but in England. An English inventor, George Stephenson, had developed the first "traveling engine," or locomotive. In 1814, a five-ton steam engine designed by Stephenson had managed to pull eight wagons up a slight incline at the modest rate of four miles per hour.

Eleven years later, in 1825, Stephenson constructed the world's first railway, England's Stockton & Darlington line. In that same year, Colonel John Stevens of New Jersey built the first American steam engine, modeled after Stephenson's locomotive.

Neither Stevens's locomotive nor the news of Stephenson's railway created much of a stir in America. The federal govern-

Theodore Dehone Judah, whose vision and perseverance helped to make a reality of the dream of a transcontinental railroad

ment, private investors, and merchants were convinced that canals would be the solution to our country's transportation problems. The opening of the Erie Canal in 1825 seemed to justify such optimism, and in the late 1820s and the early part of the following decade enthusiasm for canals continued unchecked. During this period most of the private and public money needed to build railroads was invested instead in canal construction.

Despite a lack of enthusiasm, construction of short-distance railroads was begun in America. In 1830, Colonel John Stevens's two sons obtained a charter from the state of New Jersey that permitted them to construct the Camden & Amboy Railroad between New York City and Philadelphia. The little railroad prospered, with travelers paying three dollars for a seven-hour one-way trip. Soon the Camden & Amboy expanded its services, connecting with other lines through to Pittsburgh,

Above, John Stevens's early experimental railway at Hoboken, New Jersey, 1825. Below, one of the earliest locomotive designs, George Stevenson's engine, The Rocket, 1830.

Baltimore, and Washington, D.C. Other railroad lines were built during this period, including the South Canal & Railroad in South Carolina, which connected Charleston to Hamburg; the Mohawk & Hudson in New York, connecting Albany with Schenectady; and the Baltimore & Ohio in Maryland, which linked Baltimore with nearby Ellicott Mills.

In addition to competition from the more popular canals, technical problems hampered the development of the early railroads. The early roadbeds were too soft and early railroad bridges too weak. Sometimes, as on the Camden & Amboy, trains had trouble staying on the tracks. The first rails, constructed of wood covered by an iron strip, broke down under heavy loads. And the first wood-burning engines belched enormous quantities of smoke and sparks, which rained down on the passengers.

Railway technical engineers, however, gradually solved many of the initial problems. A mechanic for the Camden & Amboy loosened the engine's front wheels and added a cowcatcher or pilot, a triangular frame attached to the front of the locomotive, which helped keep the train on the track. Engineers for the Baltimore & Ohio followed the English railway model. They built solid and level roadbeds mounted on stone blocks and constructed sturdy bridges for their railroad, many of which are still in use today.

Competitors of the railways, however, continued to impede expansion. The worst situation was in New York state. The Canal Commission, controlled by Albany's powerful merchants, who were descended from early Dutch colonists, proved a formidable opponent. The commission had allies among the stage and wagon owners whose vehicles were used by travelers when the Erie Canal was frozen over. Innkeepers and tavern owners along the overland routes also opposed the development of any alternate means of transportation. This powerful coalition of merchants, stage and wagon owners, innkeepers, and tavern owners was able to

The "West Point," the Second Locomotive built in the United States for actual service on a Railroad.

defeat most attempts to raise funds for railroad construction. Some towns went so far as to pass local ordinances banning steam engines from entering.

In the rest of the Northeast, and in the South, opposition was not as strong and the railroads quickly increased their rate of expansion. The early railroads were closely linked to the canal system. In the 1840s, most of the railways were feeder lines to water transportation systems such as the Erie Canal. Trains hauled freight to a river or canal, on which it was then transported to its final destination.

By the 1850s, though shipments to waterways still dominated, trunk lines—major railroad lines—had begun to develop. These trunk lines linked major cities, such as New York and Boston. Shorter side lines along the main routes fed into these major trunk lines.

Despite the rapid increase in railroad construction, various problems continued to impede the consolidation of major lines. One serious problem until 1886, when a standard for all lines was established, was that different railroads often had different gauges—different widths of track. These gauges were often incompatible, and trains using one line often had to unload and transfer passengers and freight at a juncture with another line rather than simply switching to the other track and continuing on the journey.

Another problem was that of how to raise the immense sums of money needed for railway construction. The majority of railway owners could not do it on their own. They needed help, but from where and in what form would it be forthcoming?

In spite of these handicaps, though, the railways had caught up to, if not surpassed, other modes of travel—as illustrated by the increase in miles of track built between 1840 and 1860. By 1840, 2,818 miles of track had been laid. By 1850, nearly 7,000 more miles had been completed. By the end of the 1860s, approximately 30,000 miles of railroad track crisscrossed the nation. In fact, by the 1860s, America was clearly in the grip of "railway fever."

The reasons for the railroads' new popularity were clear—trains were faster and cheaper than any form of transport. Merchants had been the first to catch on. Boston businessmen learned, for example, that the rates charged by the new railroad for transport of goods to nearby Worcester were one-third of the cost of shipping by wagons to the same destination. Baltimore businessmen discovered that the Baltimore & Ohio railway charged twenty-five percent less for freight than the turnpikes. Merchants in upper New York state began to realize that while barges traveled at the rate of four miles per hour downstream on the canal, trains could cover the same distance in much less time. And trains could run in any weather, while the canal was closed whenever its waters were frozen.

More popular than the less efficient steamboats (like the one in the background), the new railroads were growing rapidly. At right, suggested list of equipment needed for a four-man expedition to the gold fields

Merchants everywhere made another startling discovery: railroads were helping to facilitate business and to open new markets. Perishables such as fruit and milk could now be moved over long distances. Raw materials and manufactured goods could be transported by the railways in large quantities that had previously been too costly to ship over long distances—a development crucial to the agricultural and industrial expansion of the nation.

The expansion of the railroads provided an important next step in the industrial development that had already begun in this country. New England mill owners realized that trains could carry factory-made products such as shoes and textiles quickly and cheaply to the South and to the new markets in the West. Farmers and

INTRODUCTION.

It was not the intention of the compilers of this map to add a Guide, but from the numerous incidents which have lately sprung up regarding the Gold fields of Western Kansas, they found it impossible to lay down the location of every place which they deemed useful without rendering the topographical part crowded and indistinct. They have therefore introduced a few pages, giving the neccessary outfit for four men, six months in the mines; the distances to the principal camping places along the routes; and also the different mail stations &c. along the route to California.

List of outfits for four men six months.

TEAM, WAGON AND FIXTURES:

2 Yoke of Oxen · · · · · · · · ·	$120.00
1 Wagon · · · · · · · · · · · ·	65.00
Wagon- Cover, Yokes and chains · · · · · · · · · · · · ·	10.00
	$195.00

TOOLS:

4 Steel Picks with handles	$5.00
4 Shovels · · · · · · · · · · ·	3.00
1 Pit Saw · · · · · · · · · ·	7.00
2 Axes · · · · · · · · · · ·	2.00
1 Hatchet · · · · · · · · · ·	65
1 Saw File · · · · · · · · ·	25
2 Gold Pans · · · · · · · · ·	1.50
1 Chisel · · · · · · · · · ·	30
1 Auger · · · · · · · · · ·	25
1 Hand Saw · · · · · · · ·	1.00
1 Drawing Knife · · · · · · ·	50
25 ℔ of Nails @ 5cts. · · · ·	1.25
2 Gimlets · · · · · · · · ·	15
2 ℔ Quicksilver and retort	3.00
Sheet Iron for Long Toms	75
	$26.60

CAMP FIXTURES AND FURNITURE:

8 Pair of Blankets · · · · ·	$24.00
1 Camp Kettle · · · · · · · ·	1.00
4 Tin Plates · · · · · · · · ·	30
4 Spoons · · · · · · · · · ·	15
1 Coffee Pot · · · · · · · · ·	50
1 Camp Stand · · · · · · · ·	1.00
4 Cups · · · · · · · · · · ·	35
1 Dipper · · · · · · · · · ·	15
1 Large Spoon · · · · · · · ·	15
1 Large Fork · · · · · · · ·	15

1 Frying Pan · · · · · · · · · ·	35
1 Dutch Oven · · · · · · · · ·	70
1 Bread Pan · · · · · · · · ·	30
1 Coffee Mill · · · · · · · · ·	40
1 Wooden Bucket · · · · · · ·	25
4 Knives · · · · · · · · · · ·	1.00
	$30.75

PROVISIONS:

6 Sacks of Flour at $3 · · ·	$18.00
400 ℔ of Bacon at 10cts. · ·	40.00
100 ℔ of Coffee at 11cts.	11.00
6 ℔ of Tea at 75cts. · · · · · ·	4.50
100 ℔ of Sugar at 7cts. · · ·	7.00
100 ℔ of Salt · · · · · · · · ·	1.00
6 ℔ Ground Pepper · · · · · ·	1.00
1 Ten Gallon Water Keg	1.00
2 Bushels of Dried Fruit	2.50
2 Bushels of Beans · · · · · ·	2.00
250 ℔ Pilot Bread @ 5cts.	12.50
25 ℔ of Rice · · · · · · · · · ·	1.50
1 Box of Soap · · · · · · · · ·	1.00
	$103.00
Team	195.50
Tools	26.60
Camp Fixtures	30.75
	$355.85

SUNDRIES:

3 Gallons of Brandy,
12 ℔ Gunpowder,
25 ℔ of Lead,
10 ℔ of Shot,
2000 Gun Caps,
2 dozen Box of Matches,
15 ℔ of Candles,
1 Whet Stone,
30 ℔ of Rosin.

15

producers in the South and West could easily and profitably ship wheat, cotton, wool, and leather to the factories and markets of the Northeast.

Once the benefits to industry became obvious, pressure for the development of railroads increased enormously. Railroad fever continued to rise as settlers pushed farther westward. In 1848, after an unsuccessful revolution, thousands of Germans left their homeland and emigrated to the United States; many were farmers, who settled in the Midwest. Large numbers of Irish immigrants, driven from their homeland by famine, arrived in America shortly thereafter. Farmers from New England, discouraged by the hardships of tilling their often-poor soil, joined the immigrants on the westward trek, lured by tales of the rich, black prairie soil.

Farther west, gold had been discovered. The first big strike, in the late 1840s, was followed by a second about ten years later. In Nevada, the Comstock Lode alone yielded gold and silver worth three million dollars. Thousands of pioneers with dreams of great wealth pushed westward in pursuit of the precious metals. Would-be miners swarmed over the expanses of California, Nevada, and Colorado. Cities sprang up overnight. In 1858, Denver, Colorado, wasn't even a town. Two years later, the burgeoning settlement had its own lending library, two newspapers, and a theater.

Trade with the rapidly expanding settlements of the West was the glittering prize for which manufacturers and merchants of the three great eastern ports—New York, Boston and Baltimore—competed. Since railways provided the fastest and cheapest means of transport to the western markets, each city began to extend its railway system farther and farther west. In 1852, the Baltimore & Ohio pushed its tracks southwest to Wheeling, West Virginia, and became the first railroad to reach the Ohio River, gateway to the Midwest and the West. Shortly thereafter, the Western Railroad of Massachusetts extended its track along a northern route until its trains could travel to Montreal, Canada. With northerly and southerly routes staked out by its rivals, the New York Central Railroad ran its new tracks in between, straight to Chicago, Illinois.

In the southern states, too, steps were taken in the 1850s toward the creation of a network of railway lines. Railroads were built from Richmond in Virginia, Charleston in South Carolina, and New Orleans in Louisiana to Memphis, Tennessee and Atlanta, Georgia. By the end of the decade, Atlanta had emerged as the South's most important railway center. Even with the rapid acceleration in railroad construction during this period, however, the South was still far behind the North and the West in the development of railways.

By 1860, a series of trunk and branch railway lines criss-crossed America, from Maine to Iowa, from Chicago to Atlanta. The lands of the Far West, which had been

acquired during the 1840s through treaties and military actions, were not yet divided into states. The expansion of the railroad would provide the means to open up these territories for settlement and trade.

In the eastern half of the nation, rail lines were linking up, gauges were being standardized, and the cities of New York and Chicago were emerging as the two great transportation centers of America. In 1850 only 1,000 miles of track extended outward from Chicago. The state of Illinois, realizing the importance of the railway system to the development of the state, started to finance the building of more track. Though the settlers and merchants of Illinois were clamoring for more railroads, funds ran out and construction had to be suspended.

The federal government then stepped in, providing the first federal railroad land grant. Congress allocated 2,595,000 acres of land along the proposed route, to be distributed in alternate sections of public land within six miles of each side of the track for every mile of railroad built. Each section was an area of land one mile square.

The contract that was used to raise money for the construction of the Illinois Central Railroad became the model for the funding of most of the major railroads. As the railroad completed a given number of miles, usually ten or twenty, it could, under the contract, then sell bonds secured by the allocated sections of land—certificates which would earn interest for the purchaser, and could then be redeemed for full value at a date specified on the face of the certificate. It was through the sale of these bonds, issued with the land sections as collateral, that the Illinois Central Railroad was able to raise sufficient funds to continue the building of the railway line.

In return for the federal government's assistance, the Illinois Central Railroad had certain obligations. The railroad was

Two depictions of the young and booming railroad industry

Sherman's troops tear up rails to hinder Confederate troop movements.

to be completed in seven years. The company had to pay to the state of Illinois in perpetuity (for all time) seven percent of its gross earnings (monies earned before taxes or expenses). And finally, the United States government retained the right to regulate the fees the railroad could charge the government for the transportation of mail or federal troops.

The Illinois Central Railroad completed the seven hundred miles of track called for in the contract in 1856, three days before the seven-year deadline.

In 1859, although the railroads were gradually linking different regions of the nation, transportation west of the Mississippi River was still very limited. Few railways ventured beyond the Mississippi, forcing travelers to rely on other forms of transportation. The first stage coach routes became operational in the 1850s. The Overland Express traveled across Texas and through the New Mexico territory, then headed up along the coast of California. Making such a journey was expensive and exhausting: a traveler who left Mississippi for California had to reserve a seat ten days in advance, pay a fare of two hundred dollars (a great deal of money at that time) and spend twenty grueling days enduring a ride through undeveloped territory, where lodgings along the route were often found to be more primitive than comfortable.

The harrowing journey across the new frontier made many see clearly the need for a transcontinental railroad, which would make the trip faster, safer and much more comfortable. In response to the pressure for a coast-to-coast railway system, the federal government surveyed possible routes across the West, but no contracts were forthcoming. Rivalry between the North and the South was largely to blame. Before long, this rivalry burst into flame: from 1861 to 1865 America was in the throes of the Civil War.

By the spring of 1861, the Union and Confederate armies began to tear up railroad track as they retreated and to rebuild

The mounting of this cannon on a flatbed car was typical of the Union Army's innovative use of the railroads.

it only for their own purposes as they advanced. In heavily contested areas, large sections of track became unusable for many months as the process of destroying and rebuilding went on.

During the Civil War the railroads were important not only for their use in covering retreats or facilitating troop advances. In a larger sense, it became apparent that whichever side controlled the most track would control the course of the war, for control of the track meant controlling the means to transport necessary supplies. It also meant controlling the means to transport large numbers of troops over great distances. The North, with twice as much existing railroad track as the South, many more operational trains, and superior track, equipment and personnel, had a clear advantage over the South.

To break the siege of Chattanooga in 1863, the North sent 25,000 men over 1,000 miles of track in just 12 days, an extraordinarily short time then for such a task. In 1864, General William Tecumseh Sherman led 100,000 Northern troops through Georgia to Atlanta. To provision Sherman's forces, 30,000 animals and huge amounts of supplies were transported over 427 miles of Northern-controlled track. Sherman later admitted that without the railroads and the engineers in charge of track construction and repairs, "the successful drive through Georgia might not have been possible."

As the Civil War continued, the importance of the railroads increased, as control of existing track proved over and over to be a key battle factor. Once again, the idea of the Great Continental Railroad was put forth. This time the government was prepared to do more than survey some land. This time the government would listen to Theodore Judah.

On the bank, General Haupt, Commander of the U.S. Military Railroad Construction Corps (in long coat and hat), supervises the digging of an embankment.

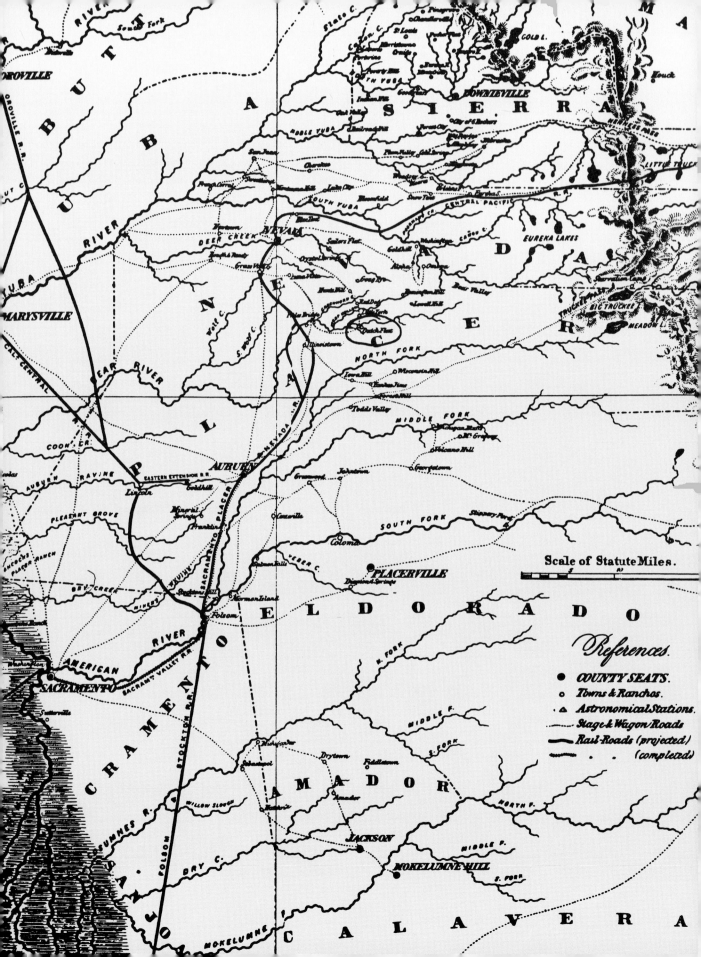

2

JUDAH'S DREAM

In 1854, after a land and sea journey of several months, Theodore Judah and his young wife arrived in California from the Northeast. The twenty-seven-year-old engineer had been hired to chart, and then build, a short railroad from the California state capital at Sacramento to the foothills of the Sierra Nevada mountain range.

To reach Sacramento from the East, the Judahs had traveled on steamboats and crossed Central America by land, though they could have used any one of several other modes of transportation to get from the one coast to the other. They could have, for example, sailed around Cape Horn, at the tip of South America; or they could have crossed the mountains and prairies of the American continent in either a horse-drawn coach or as part of a wagon train. All of these methods of transportation, including the one chosen by the Ju-

dahs, involved a journey of several months and were dangerous as well as most uncomfortable.

When the Judahs finally set foot on California soil, Theodore Judah had a mission—or as some said, an obsession. He wanted to build a railroad from the Sierras eastward across the continent.

Theodore Judah was not the first to dream of a "Great Transcontinental." In 1845, Connecticut's Asa Whitney had suggested to Congress that it set aside for such a purpose a sixty-mile-wide strip of land from the Mississippi River to the Columbia River. Before the Civil War, Army engineers had surveyed possible railroad routes across the West. Nothing further had come of it, largely because of the sectional rivalry between the North and the South. Each area wanted the great road to pass through territories under its control.

Theodore Judah may not have been the first man to propose a transcontinental railroad, but he was certainly a great

Map of central California, 1860, showing several railroads, the town of Dutch Flat, and the city of Sacramento.

promoter of the idea. Everywhere he went in California he sold the idea of a Pacific railroad. He was so tireless in his efforts that he soon became known as "Crazy Judah." Enough Californians believed in him, however, to send the young man to Washington, D.C., to lobby for federal support for a transcontinental railroad.

Judah's mission to Washington was unsuccessful. People were interested, but the capital was preoccupied with the issue of slavery and the secession of the South from the Union. Judah returned to California, vowing, "the railway will be built and I'm going to have something to do with it."

Theodore Judah decided that the people in Washington might be swayed in favor of the transcontinental railroad if he provided for them more exact cost estimates and a possible route. In the summer of 1860 Judah set off for the Sierra Nevadas to find that route. He found it between the Donner and Emigrant passes, which had each been made famous on their own by earlier wagon trains. That autumn, in the mining town of Dutch Flat, California, Judah drew up the Articles of Association of the Central Pacific Railroad of California.

The next step was to raise money to build the 115 miles of railway from Sacramento to Nevada. To be incorporated in California, the Cental Pacific had to obtain pledges of at least one thousand dollars for each proposed mile of track.

Charles Crocker

After unsuccessful attempts to raise money in San Francisco, Judah tried in the city of Sacramento. In June, 1861, he unfolded part of his dream to a dozen or so men seated in a room above a local hardware store. Saying nothing about a transcontinental railroad, Judah spoke only about a short line to move Sacramento goods to the new mining camps in Nevada.

Four of the men present listened with special attention. One was Leland Stanford, a wholesale grocer. Another was a dry goods salesman named Charles Crocker. The other two, Mark Hopkins and his partner Collis Huntington, owned the hardware store where the meeting took place.

After the meeting, the four men decided to back Judah. They incorporated their enterprise, making themselves officers of the corporation. And they sent Theodore

Mark Hopkins

Collis P. Huntington

Judah back to Washington, D.C., to seek federal aid for their enterprise. Little did the men know that this decision would change not only their lives but the history of the nation.

Theodore Judah fared better on his second trip to Washington. The Civil War had begun, and the federal government wanted to link itself more closely to the territories in the Far West. A transcontinental railroad would make the vast agricultural and mineral resources of the interior available to the federal war effort.

In 1862, Congress had passed the Homestead Act, which provided for the sale of uninhabited lands. These lands were sold in parcels of 160 acres, for very low prices, with the provision that the purchaser live and work on the homestead thus created. If homesteaders were to easily reach their new lands, move needed supplies and bring in manufactured goods from the East, a network of railroads would have to be built in the West.

In that same year, 1862, President Abraham Lincoln signed the Pacific Railroad Act. It provided that two railroad companies—one from the east and one from the west—should build the Pacific Railroad. The name of the eastern company was the Union Pacific, which was to lay track westward from Omaha, Nebraska. The Central Pacific would start from Sacramento, California, and lay track eastward. The Pacific Railroad Act decreed that the two tracks meet near the California-Nevada boundary line, at a point to be determined at a later date.

The Pacific Railroad Act provided enough financial aid for the building of the transcontinental railroad. Each company received a 400-foot-wide right-of-way strip

National Portrait Gallery

Abraham Lincoln, sixteenth president of the United States

26

A popular, if romantic, representation of the transcontinental route.

and 10 land sections per mile, 5 alternate land sections on each side of the track. These were federally owned lands, granted to the companies by the government. Once the railroads began construction, they could sell these lands to raise money for more construction.

In addition to the land grants, the Pacific Railroad Act stipulated that Congress would loan money to the railroad construction companies for every mile of track put down. The loans were given in the form of low-interest bonds, to be paid back in thirty years. The bonds were issued on a scale of construction difficulty. In the flatlands, the railroads were loaned 16,000 dollars per mile. In the mountains, where the work was the hardest, they received 48,000 dollars per mile. In the plateaus between, they were issued loans of 32,000 dollars per mile.

Theodore Judah wired the good news to his partners in Sacramento: "We have drawn the elephant. Now let us see if we can harness him up."

On his return, however, Judah's triumph turned sour. In his absence his partners had begun to shove him aside. Moreover, they had been employing some questionable business practices. In 1861, Leland Stanford had been elected governor of California. Using his new power and prestige, Stanford attempted to squeeze more money from the federal

As the end of the nineteenth century approached, railroads spanned the rivers and prairies of America, insuring the settlement and development of the Western states.

government for construction loans by finding experts willing to swear that the foothills of the Sierras began nearer to Sacramento than they actually did. If the government agreed with these estimates, it would have to loan the Central Pacific more money, because the railroad would then cross more mountainous land (at 48,000 dollars per mile) than had been previously estimated. Ignorant of western geography, federal government officials went along with the new estimate.

Leland Stanford wasn't the only one whose actions angered Theodore Judah on his return to Sacramento. When construction of the railroad began in 1863, Charles Crocker contracted to build the road at great profit to himself and the three other partners of his new construction company. These three partners just happened to be Stanford, Hopkins, and Huntington, the chief officers of the Central Pacific. The owners of the railroad were paying themselves to build the railroad. Even worse, they were paying themselves more than the cost of the construction.

The "Big Four" of the Central Pacific soon bought out the dissatisfied Theodore Judah. He was paid 100,000 dollars for his shares of Central Pacific stock. Judah returned to the East, probably to gain backing for an attempt to regain control of the Central Pacific. But his plans were cut short. On his way back East, Judah contracted a fever while crossing the Isthmus of Panama. He died shortly after reaching New York. Sixty years after his death, a small statue of Judah was erected in Sacramento, the city to which he had gone with his dream of a transcontinental railroad.

3

THE GREAT RACE

The great railroad race to complete a transcontinental line began slowly, at least for the Union Pacific. The company started laying track in 1863, but by May of 1866 the railroad had advanced only forty miles out of Omaha. This dismal situation changed for the better with the arrival of a new chief engineer, General Grenville Dodge.

Dodge had become famous during the Civil War, as a railroad engineer for the Union side. Under his command, for example, at one time during the war 100 miles of track and 182 bridges had been rebuilt in only 40 days.

After the war, General Dodge had been sent out West to lead the military campaign against Native Americans of the Plains tribes. While pushing these tribes from the areas surrounding the proposed railroad, Dodge looked for passes with grades (slopes) gentle enough so that railroad tracks to cross them could be built with relatively little difficulty.

When Dodge took over the construction of the railroad, his military experience paid off. By the end of 1866, when winter halted construction temporarily at North Platte, Nebraska, 280 miles of track had been laid—240 under Dodge's supervision. Dodge's two construction bosses, Jack and Dan Casement, contributed substantially to his success. Under the management of the Casement brothers, the Union Pacific construction force of 1,000 men had been efficiently organized, divided into groups of workers with specific tasks which were coordinated to function cooperatively.

First came the surveying parties, each escorted by a small band of soldiers. Surveying parties worked hundreds of miles ahead of the construction crews, laying out and marking the route over which the tracks would be built. These parties were followed by the location men, who staked out the exact grades and curves. Next came the grading crews, whose job it was

General Grenville Dodge, chief engineer for the Union Pacific Railroad

31

to soften the inclines and level the ground over which the rails were to be laid. To feed and supply these crews, which worked so far ahead of the track layers, wagons hauled enormous amounts of beef and equipment over hundreds of miles.

The bridge builders worked closer to the track crews. They had to work fast, or the construction of the track would be delayed. This extreme pressure often resulted in problems later on; some bridges built in haste were flimsily constructed.

The last crews along the route were the track layers. To assist these crews, the Casement brothers had devised a twenty-car work train, which resembled a miniature city. The train contained kitchens, offices, carpentry and machine shops, a general store, feed stores, and dormitories with bunks for sleeping. Since the plains over which the tracks were being laid yielded no wood, iron, or food (the men wouldn't eat buffalo meat), these supplies had to be transported from the East to Omaha and from there over a single line of track out to the crews.

The track crews functioned in a manner similar to an assembly line in a factory. First, a supply train dumped construction materials—ties, rails and spikes. These were then loaded on flatcars and moved to the last finished track along the newly laid line. To build the track, for each length of rail five ties were set down. Once the ties were in place, on command five men on either side of the track lifted the two 500-

Left page, top, this california and Oregon Coast Railroad survey crew was typical of the crews used on the transcontinental route. Middle, track crew of the Union Pacific in Nebraska, 1866. Bottom, construction crew poses in front of supply train, 1868.

Below, triple decker dormitory cars on the St. Paul, Minneapolis & Manitoba Railroad, circa 1890, were similar to those used on the first transcontinental line.

pound rails and dropped them into place. The clampers and spikers fastened down the rails, ten strokes to a spike, ten spikes to a rail. Then the flatcar moved ahead. A mile of track was made up of 400 of these rails; by the end of 1866, the Union Pacific's track crew was laying about a mile a day. The Casement brothers offered the crews double pay if two miles of track a day could be laid. Soon the crews were up to two miles a day, or even three.

The men on the Union Pacific crews were a mixed lot. There were veterans of service on both sides in the Civil War, many of whom still wore their faded Confederate grays or Union blues. Working alongside the veterans were mule skinners, gamblers, failed miners and immigrants from the East. Most of the immigrants on the crews were Irish-Americans.

The crewmen were a tough lot, and they had to be. The conditions under which they worked were extremely harsh. One ex-workman later recalled the lice and the bedbugs that infested everything. The weather also offered some nasty surprises. Torrential rains fell out of the summer sky of the plains, and in the spring of 1867, record rains washed away miles of track and bridges in Nebraska.

The Native Americans of the Plains tribes, recognizing the extension of the railroads as a threat to their way of life, became a serious threat to the railroad workers. The railroad would bring a life of settlement, homesteaders from the East, private land ownership, and fixed boundaries to the plains. This was directly opposed to the way of life of the Plains tribes, hunters and gatherers who for cen-

Buffalo hunt on the plains.

turies had crossed and re-crossed the open plains following the migration of vast herds of buffalo. The buffalo provided food, clothing, and even shelter for the tribespeople, whose homes were constructed of buffalo hides and saplings—portable structures that could be packed up and taken along when the buffalo were again on the move. The buffalo was the central figure in the folklore and religion of the Plains tribes. The reduction of the vast expanses of open plains, which had come with the construction of the railroads, was beginning to destroy the great buffalo herds upon which the Apache, the Sioux, the Cheyenne and other Plains tribes relied for their very existence. Seeing the "Iron Horse" destroying their way of life, the proud warriors of the plains fought back with all their strength, ingenuity, and resources.

The surveying crews of the Union Pacific worked under hazardous conditions as they moved farther west. Far away from the main bodies of the Union Pacific crews, they were often also far away from military garrisons which might afford them some protection from hostile warrior bands. At best, small squads of cavalry were dispatched to accompany them. So, like most of the other Union Pacific workmen on the westward crews, members of the advance parties carried guns and rifles with which to protect themselves.

In 1866, Native American tribes attacked the railway crews. The first violence came at Plum Creek, about 200 miles west of Omaha. A Sioux raiding party captured the crew of a stalled train. The operator of a nearby telegraph station saw the attack and wired the main camp at Plum Creek. General Dodge, who had been inspecting the work at the end of the track, boarded another train and raced to the rescue with twenty volunteers. The Sioux galloped away without any further show of force, but this small incident signaled the beginning of twenty months of warfare.

The Army and the Union Pacific worked closely together to subdue the Plains tribes. The Army needed the railway in order to protect the new settlements in the West. Transported by train, troops could go quickly to the rescue from far away. As for General Dodge, he also needed the soldiers to protect his men. "They want to see occasionally a soldier to give them confidence, and that is all we need to get labor on the line," he wrote to General William Sherman. In reply, Sherman promised, "every man I can get and spare."

In the spring of 1867, the Plains tribes stepped up their attacks on the railway crews. On May 25th, a Sioux war party killed five men in a section gang at Overton, Nebraska. Later the same day, about one hundred miles to the west, Sioux warriors killed four graders working on the tracks. Other incidents followed, but despite these dangers work on the railroads continued.

The management of the Union Pacific

The Fall of the Native American Nations

"Tell General Howard I know his heart.... I am tired of fighting. Our chiefs are killed.... The old men are all dead.... It is cold and we have no blankets. The little children are freezing to death. My people, some of them, have run away to the hills, and have no blankets, no food; no one knows where they are — perhaps freezing to death. I want to have time to look for my children and see how many of them I can find. Maybe I shall find them among the dead. Hear me, my chiefs! I am tired; my heart is sick and sad. From where the sun now stands, I will fight no more forever."

Heinmot Tooyalaket
Chief Joseph of the Nez Perce

These words signaled the end of a proud and vital Native American civilization which had thrived in the forests, plains and mountains of this country for centuries. The eastern nations were the first defeated by the unstoppable tide of immigration from Europe, and by the 1860s, when the last great Indian Wars occurred, these nations were either extinct or confined to reservations usually far from their homelands.

The final conquest of the Native American Nations began in the southwest, where the great Apache chief Cochise led his warriors and their families in a precarious, fly-by-night existence for almost twenty years. They survived by hunting the scarce game and by raiding the white settlers who had invaded their homeland for cattle and horses. Finally, in 1872, Cochise's perseverence and determination that his people should not leave the land of their fathers paid off. He and his tribe were allotted a reservation in the Chiricahua Mountains for which their tribe was named. Other Apache tribes were not so lucky. Many were sent to far off reservations. And in a raid by treacherous white settlers from the Tucson region, one tribe was nearly wiped out.

In the North, the Sioux, with assistance from allied tribes of Arapahoe and Cheyenne, were beginning a last brave battle for the Black Hills and Powder River Basin of North Dakota and Montana. These lands were sacred to these Native American nations, the heart of their culture. When the government tried to force upon the tribes a sale of their lands, they decided they had no choice but to fight. After losing the Battle of Rosebud, 264 soldiers from the U.S. Seventh Cavalry, under the leadership of General George Armstrong Custer, attacked a site along the Little Bighorn River, where over 2500 Sioux, Arapaho and Cheyenne warriors, with their wives and children, were camped. The soldiers' cold-blooded murder of women and children so incensed the warriors that they surrounded Custer's army and killed the U.S. troops, to a man.

It was a Pyhrric victory for the Sioux tribes; hunted by the U.S. Army, they were forced to run and hide in the mountains where, unable to hunt buffalo or set up camp, they found themselves freezing and starving to death. Sitting Bull led his tribe north to safety in Canada, while Crazy Horse was forced to surrender his people to the U.S. Troops. Crazy Horse, taken prisoner, was murdered at Fort Robinson, Montana.

The Nez Perce had been friends to the white man as far back as Lewis and Clark, whom they had aided and sheltered. Told they must leave their homeland for a reservation, they began the journey peacefully. But some young braves killed four white settlers who were attempting to steal some Nez Perce horses. Thus began a 1000-mile running conflict, during which 300 Nez Perce warriors, burdened with women, children and household goods, managed to elude not one but two United States armies. Finally, just 50 miles from the Canadian border and safety, finding themselves in a blizzard and surrounded by enemy troops, Chief Joseph and the Nez Perce surrendered.

The captured Native American Nations were doomed to an existence of poverty and disease at the hands of corrupt and incompetent officials on reservations far from their homelands. Many of the northern nations were sent to "Indian Territory," a vast, barren area in what is now the state of Oklahoma.

It is to the great credit of the Native American Nations that they have managed to survive a century of abuse and neglect with their languages and cultures relatively intact. Their way of life has been irreparably damaged, but many tribes have sued successfully for retribution, and reinstatment of tribal lands lost through fraud. Many have developed industries and re-established tribal government on their reservations. It was once thought that the Native Americans were a "dying species," but the presence of vital Native American communities throughout the 50 states disproves this prophecy.

permitted the construction of a temporary town after the completion of every sixty miles of track, as an incentive for the crews. Each town had shacks for the workers, saloons, dance halls and gambling tents. After a new stretch of track was completed, the town was torn down. The wood was loaded on flatcars and moved along the new track to the site of the "next" town. Many of the railroad workers spent much of their pay amusing themselves in these temporary towns along the Union Pacific route.

The Union Pacific track moved swiftly west because the construction process was so well organized and because much of the land the track had crossed was flat, which made progress relatively easy. In 1868, however, 3,000 men found themselves working in three-foot-deep snow in the Medicine Bow Mountains of Wyoming.

Although the snow was troublesome, General Dodge was optimistic about achieving the year's construction goal—the completion of 400 miles of track. He hoped that a federal commission set up to deal with the Native Americans would be able to negotiate a new peace. If the commission failed, the Army had 5,000 troops patrolling the area between Omaha and the Salt Lake Valley, which could be called upon to protect the railroad crews.

Ahead of the construction crews stretched the Laramie Plains of Wyoming. To the east and to the west rose the Rocky Mountains. The Union Pacific route stretched

Bear River City, near what is now the Utah-Wyoming border, was typical of the ramshackle towns that followed the track crews as they moved westward.

across the Plains to Salt Lake Valley.

Dodge drove his construction crews particularly hard that summer. Before the end of July, 1868, the forward base was at Benton, Utah, 700 miles west of Omaha. Before autumn, graders were beyond Salt Lake City.

The Central Pacific Railroad, when it began construction, faced different problems than those of its rival. Unlike the crews of the Union Pacific, Central Pacific crews had to immediately confront the task of laying track over a mountain range. The Sierra Nevadas presented a formidable challenge.

The Central Pacific had problems assembling a construction crew. In California there were no large groups of recent European immigrants like the Irish who formed such a large portion of the Union Pacific crews. The largest immigrant group in California was the Chinese, thousands of whom had emigrated during the Gold Rush of the late 1840s.

At an average weight of 110 pounds, the Chinese were considered too small and frail to work on the railroad. By reminding his colleagues that the Chinese had built the Great Wall, Charles Crocker, head of construction for the Central Pacific, convinced his partners to give the Chinese a chance to work for the railroad. Stanford,

Hopkins and Huntington (the other members of the Central Pacific's "Big Four," along with Crocker) agreed reluctantly, but were soon convinced of the abilities of the Chinese workers. By 1865, 2,000 Chinese workers were employed on the Central Pacific, and recruiters had gone to Canton, on the Chinese mainland, to recruit another 4,000 workers.

Like most immigrants, the Chinese laborers worked long, hard hours for little pay. They had one advantage, however, over their Caucasian counterparts: in boiling the water for their tea and rice, the Chinese workers avoided many of the diseases that plagued the other crewmen on the railroads.

Prejudice was a major problem that confronted the Chinese crewmen. Their fellow workers, many of them Irish-Americans, objected to working alongside the "heathen Chinese," who were not Christians. They objected even more strongly to the physically slighter Chinese being paid the same wage, and after a crew of Caucasian track layers threatened to strike, the Central Pacific instituted a discriminatory wage scale that remained in effect for the duration of the construction.

By late autumn of 1866, Central Pacific crews had pushed ninety-four miles east of Sacramento. Snow began falling in the

Left page, top, Burning Rock Cut, 1866, made by the Union Pacific crews, was named after a night watchman accidentally set the oil shale walls on fire. Middle, Heath's Ravine, 1867, on the Central Pacific Line, is an example of the extensive grading used in the mountains. Bottom, Owl Gap Cut, 1866, on the Central Pacific line, illustrates the stages of cutting.

Above, Newcastle Trestle, built in 1864, was typical of the quickly constructed wooden trestles and bridges built by early railroad crews. Below left, snowshed under construction near Summit, California. Below right, snowshed interior.

Snowsheds at entrance to Tunnel No. 6, Summit, California

mountains during early October. Nevertheless, work continued, even in fifteen-foot-deep snow. It took five locomotives to push one snow plow through the massive drifts. Avalanches swept crewmen away; one entire camp was buried in this manner.

There was also the problem of digging tunnels through granite hills. Workers dug seven tunnels within one two-mile stretch. The worst of these was the quarter-mile-long Summit Tunnel, which took an entire year to complete. Crews working side by side managed to chip away only eight inches of granite a day.

For a short time the Central Pacific construction crews experimented with a new explosive to facilitate the tunneling—nitroglycerin. Though powerful, the unstable nitroglycerin caused frequent accidents, and the workers were ordered to stop using it.

While their crews labored in the moun-

Train entering snowshed, 1890.

Central Pacific crews laying track in the Nevada desert, 1869

"Driving of the Last Spike," by Thomas Hill.

tains, the Big Four worried about the Union Pacific. Construction on the rival railway line was proceeding rapidly; if the Central Pacific did not pick up its pace, the two railroads would meet at the Nevada border. To have to stop at the border would be a disaster for the Central Pacific, for it was estimated that a railroad reaching only to the border would be lightly used. The real money would come only if the Central Pacific pushed on across the deserts of Nevada into Utah.

Recruitment for the Central Pacific crews was stepped up. By 1867, there were 12,000 men, most of whom were Chinese, working on the 40-mile stretch from the summit to the eastern base of the Sierras. With this influx of additional labor it was possible for the crews to work night and day, in shifts.

During June, 1868, the Central Pacific finally reached the Nevada border. Once out of the mountains, the pace of construction quickened. The Chinese laborers were working under the broiling sun of the Nevada plains, often under brutal and inhumane conditions, as Crocker pushed his crews ever harder. His goal was "a mile of track for every working day"—for every mile of track completed east of the Nevada border would be worth hundreds of thousands of dollars to the backers of the Central Pacific.

Where were the Native Americans who had so plagued the Union Pacific? Although there were tribes along the Central Pacific's route, they gave the railroad little trouble. The men who ran the Central Pacific dealt more cautiously with the Digger, Snake, Piute, and Shoshone tribes

than the Union Pacific had done with the endangered and hostile tribes of the Plains. The Central Pacific even negotiated a treaty with the Piute and the Shoshone.

Collis Huntington, the brains of the Big Four, explained one way peace was maintained: "We gave the old chiefs a pass each, good on the passenger cars, and we told our men to let the common Indians ride on the freight cars whenever they saw fit."

Without having to beat back Native American war parties, the Central Pacific raced forward during 1868. By year's end, the men had completed 362 miles of track, only 3 miles short of the Crocker's goal.

Crocker didn't let up. During the early months of 1869, the crews continued to work furiously. Crocker ordered his graders to proceed 300 miles in advance of his track layers.

Meanwhile, the grading crews of the two railroads were now working only a hundred feet apart on the slope of the Promontory Mountains. The level of hostility between the two rival crews rose steadily.

The Irish-American workers on the Union Pacific resented the fact that Chinese crewmen of the Central Pacific, whom they considered inferior to them, were doing "white man's work." The crews of the two railroads were working only a few hundred yards away from one another when the incidents of rock-throwing and pick-swinging began.

The management of both of the railroads wanted to avoid property damage, and the foremen on both sides attempted to quash the escalating violence. It wasn't until after an explosion caused "a section of the Union's line [to] mysteriously [shoot] forward," burying several Irishmen alive, that the violence finally stopped.

On May 10, 1869, with much ceremony and fanfare, the tracks of the Union Pacific and the Central Pacific met at Promontory Point in Utah. Cultural and ethnic differences were forgotten as the workers celebrated with pride. It was now possible to travel from New York to San Francisco by rail. And the West was open to settlement and trade.

"Thousand-Mile Tree." Tracklayers of the Union Pacific pose as they mark the first thousand miles of track laid from Omaha, Nebraska, 1869.

AFTER THE SHOUTING WAS OVER

Three years after the completion of the transcontinental railroad, the Credit Mobilier scandal broke. The Credit Mobilier was the construction company that built the Union Pacific Railroad. The construction company was controlled by the same men who controlled the railway—Thomas Durant and Oliver and Oakes Ames. Like the Big Four of the Central Pacific Railroad, the powers behind the Union Pacific had paid themselves to build their own railroad. And, like the Big Four, they had paid themselves far more than the actual cost of the construction.

The dishonesty of the owners of the Credit Mobilier quickly became evident to the Union Pacific's chief engineer, Peter Dey, who had estimated the cost of the track from Omaha west at 30,000 dollars per mile. Thomas Durant asked Dey to calculate his estimate on the basis of wider roadbeds and better grades. Dey raised it

to 50,000 dollars per mile. The railroad then decided to use the earlier, cheaper standard, but paid the Credit Mobilier as if the railway were to be built with wider roadbeds and better grades. The honest Dey resigned.

In an attempt to insure that the federal government would not question the policies and practices of the Credit Mobilier, Oakes Ames began to distribute Credit Mobilier stock to influential politicians at far less than face value. A member of Congress from 1863 to 1873, Ames had easy access to powerful men, many of whom accepted his offer, including Vice President Schuyler Colfax, and the Speaker of the House, James G. Blaine.

Finally, after a disgruntled insider sued the Credit Mobilier, Congress began its own investigation. In the aftermath, it censured Oakes Ames and another congressman who was an investor in the Credit Mobilier. Ames died several weeks later.

The Central Pacific's Big Four escaped a similar fate. A "mysterious" fire de-

Credit Mobilier stock certificate

The Ames brothers, Oliver (left) and Oakes (center), and the engineer Peter Dey (right).

stroyed its financial records, making an investigation of the company's dealings nearly impossible.

Though the Credit Mobilier scandal was big, it soon died down. There was another reverse, however, for the proponents of the first transcontinental railroad. Immediately after the ceremony at Promontory Point, it was announced that the Suez Canal had been completed. The builders of the transcontinental railroad had hoped to carry goods from the Far East across the continent to eastern ports, where they would then be shipped to Europe. The opening of the Suez Canal, which enabled exporters in the Far East to ship goods through the canal and over the Mediterranean Sea to Europe, meant that this dream of reaping profits from the shipping of international trade goods from the Far East would be largely unrealized by the railroads.

In addition, the volume of railway traffic had fallen off after the initial excitement had faded. After a while, the trains were transporting only light freight and a few passengers.

The situation was particularly bad for the Union Pacific, even before the Credit Mobilier scandal broke. The Union Pacific was heavily in debt, having not yet paid off its federal loans. As a result, the value of its stock dropped sharply. After the scandal, the line changed hands a number of times. The new owners were not interested in building up the shaky company; in fact, they drained its financial resources even more. After decades of bad ownership, large sections of the line needed rebuilding and improvement.

Train wreck, circa 1890. Hastily built bridges often proved dangerous in the early years of railroading.

In the years to come, the Union Pacific would not be the only western railroad to have financial problems. Spurred on by the completion of the first transcontinental railroad, the new railroads had borrowed huge sums of money for construction. As a result, most were in debt. To raise money, they resorted to a variety of illegal practices. They offered secret discounts to large investors. They each carried only a certain portion of the total volume of freight and passengers. By thus agreeing not to compete against each other, they managed to keep their rates high. These practices led to the eventual regulation of the railroads by the federal government and state governments.

In fact, the huge debt was also partially responsible for the surprisingly light traffic on the railroad shortly after the completion of the transcontinental route. The rates were simply too high. Rates remained high on western railroads until the end of the century, when passenger fares were cut in half and freight fares dipped even lower.

The building of the first transcontinental railroad had also set a standard for the construction of subsequent western railroads. To make a profit, owners built their railroads as quickly as possible, often using inferior equipment and routes. These practices resulted in a number of accidents. Only slowly did the railroads rebuild poorly

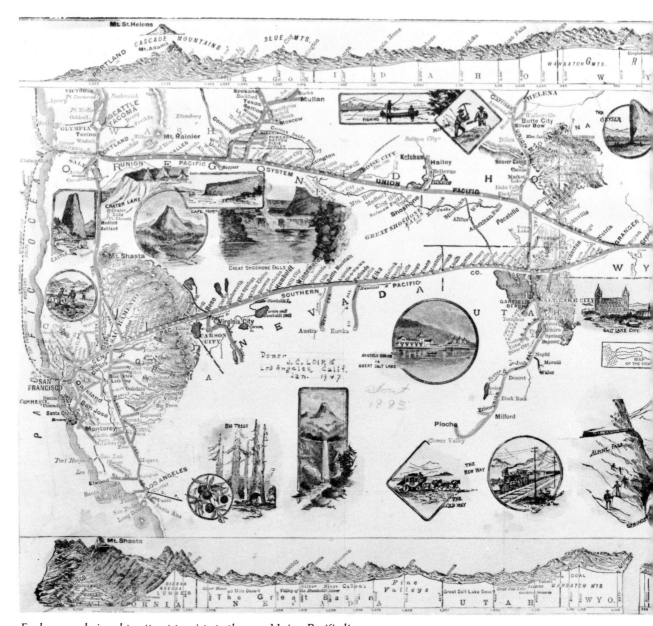

Early map, designed to attract tourists to the new Union Pacific line

constructed bridges and roadbeds. Yet railroads eventually did become safer. New signals made riding less dangerous. Steel rails replaced the old, brittle iron rails.

A spate of railroad building set off by the completion of the transcontinental line spurred a second safety problem. In the late 1860s, hold-up gangs began to rob the western trains. The gangs worked mostly in Indiana, Kentucky, Iowa, Tennessee, and Nevada. Perhaps the most famous of

these train-robbing gangs was the James gang, headed by Jesse James and his brother Frank. The James brothers pulled their first railway hold-up in 1873. Their last hold-up was in 1881. During all those years, they escaped arrest.

The railroad gangs had a fairly easy time of it. Boarding a train was a simple matter. Passengers rarely resisted. The public was rather sympathetic, because in a number of places the railroads, with their

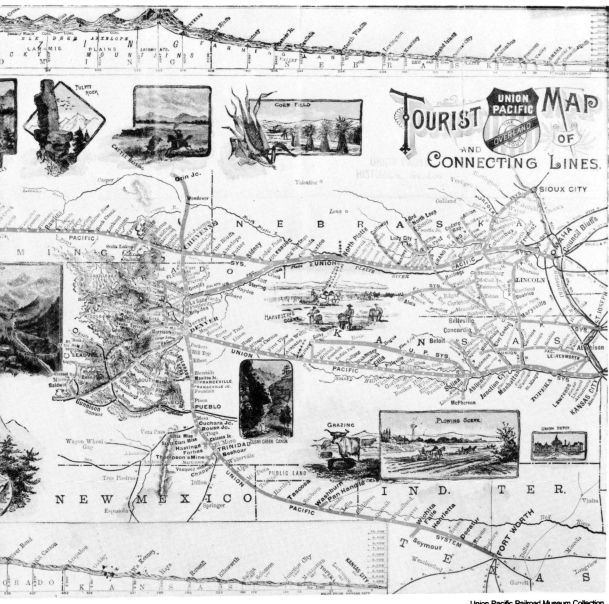

Union Pacific Railroad Museum Collection

high rates, were unpopular. The railroad gangs had a brief life, however. Faster trains, all-steel cars, and better police protection for the railroads ended the careers of the train robbers.

Scandals, debts, the low number of riders, faulty equipment, robbers—all of these were the short-term aftermath of the completion of the transcontinental railroad. Some of these effects could be directly attributed to the road. Others,

like the rise of the train-robbing gangs, were more indirect.

Some effects of the completion of the transcontinental railroad were more far-reaching and long-lasting. Abraham Lincoln had once predicted that the settlement of the Far West would take another century. The transcontinental railroad cut his estimate by half. By 1912, the last of the forty-eight continental United States had joined the Union.

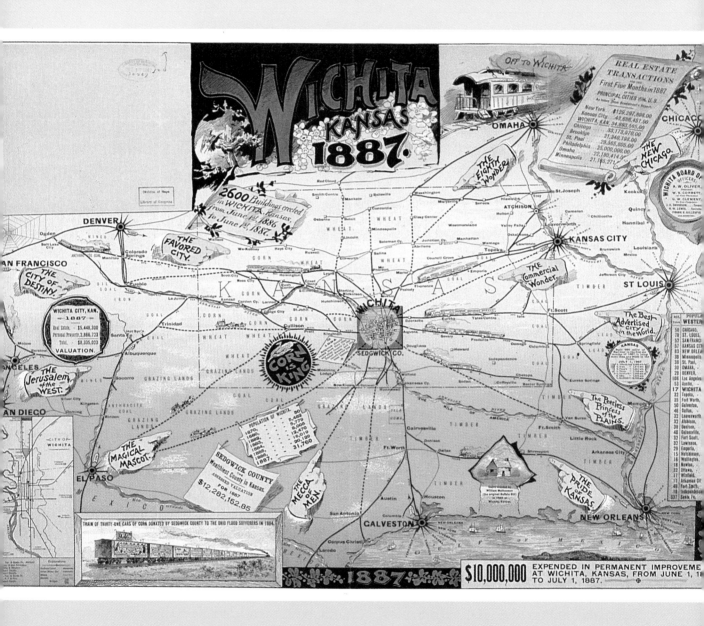

5

THE ROAD FROM PROMONTORY POINT

The railroads helped to spur the settlement of the West, but at a great cost. In 1860, the nation's prairie teemed with 13 million buffalo. As tracks were laid across the prairie, thousands of buffalo were slaughtered. Buffalo killing became quite fashionable, and passengers shot at them from the trains. By the 1870s, merchants had discovered that buffalo hides could be made into robes and used to make belts for assembly-line machines. Commercial hunters moved in, shooting the buffalo by the thousands. At the end of the century, only a few hundred buffalo remained of the once-vast herds that had roamed the plains.

Without the buffalo, which had been at the center of their entire way of life, the people of the Plains tribes could not survive on their own. Increasingly, these proud people had to depend on the federal government for food. The tragedy deep-ened as corrupt officials appointed to serve the needs of the Plains peoples lined their own pockets with the funds allocated for the support of the Native Americans in their charge.

The Plains tribes were affected by the coming of the railroads in another way, as well, which was eventually even more devastating. The opening up of the West brought to the lands of the Plains tribes settlers and miners who laid their own claims to the same territory, claims supported by the federal government. In the years 1867 and 1868, government agents demanded that the Plains tribes give up more land and move to reservations—lands which had been set aside for their relocation. These reservation lands, however, were more often than not unsuitable for such purposes. Furthermore, the way the Native Americans were assigned to the

These souvenir maps lured new settlers to the growing cities of the West.

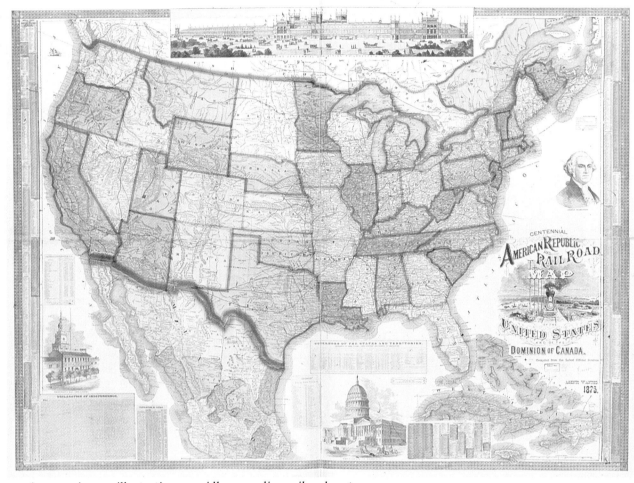

A souvenir map illustrating a rapidly expanding railroad system.

land does not now seem logical: the northern tribes were pushed farther north in the harsh territory of the Black Hills of the Dakotas, while the southern tribes and those of the Great Plains were forced onto poor lands in Oklahoma.

In 1874, conflict arose once again over lands inhabited by Native Americans—lands to which they had been relocated. Gold was discovered in the Black Hills, and thousands of miners staked claims on the reservation lands. The tribes fought back. In 1876, General George Armstrong Custer and his troops rode into the heart of the Sioux territory. At Little Big Horn, a Sioux force of 2,500 warriors destroyed Custer's troops to the last man.

The tribes fought on, but though the fierce and brave Apache held out until 1886, their struggle was in vain. One general involved in the military actions against the western tribes commented:

> We took away their country and their means of support, broke up their mode of living, their habits of life, introduced disease and death among them, and it was for this and against this that they made war. Can anyone expect less?

The building of the transcontinental railroad had another effect of lasting and sometimes painful consequence. The completion of the transcontinental line stimulated the building of other railroads throughout the territory.

By 1893, five transcontinental lines linked the West with the East—the Southern Pacific, the Northern Pacific, the Great Northern, and the Santa Fe had established routes in addition to the original transcontinental railway line. In fact, lines were being built everywhere in the West. To some observers it seemed that owners had given little thought to where they put their roads down. Often builders didn't seem to notice whether there was another railroad nearby with which to connect. The only thing that seemed to matter was constructing more and more miles of track.

To pay for this ongoing construction, the new railroads vigorously promoted settlement of the lands along their routes. Thousands of new settlers were lured to the West from the eastern states—and even from Europe—by colonizing agents for the burgeoning railroads. These settlers hardly expected the harsh life that so many of them would later endure. The colonizing agents circulated pamphlets and brochures advertising the new Eden of the American West. One Union Pacific pamphlet, for example, glowingly described the Platte Valley as, "a flowery meadow of great fertility clothed in nutritious grasses and watered by numerous streams." This

was the same valley where fierce storms had terrified the Union Pacific construction crews.

Other pamphlets described men who had gotten rich in the West. The brochures even offered marriage as an inducement to settlement. One railroad promised, "when a daughter of the East is once beyond the Missouri she rarely recrosses it except on a bridal tour." On a more practical note, the railroads promised to transport emigrants to their new lands.

The efforts of the railroads to attract settlers were extremly successful. Thousands of Scandinavians emigrated to Minnesota and the Dakotas. Many Germans and Irish left their countries for Nebraska and the Dakotas.

One railroad, the Santa Fe, even sent an agent into Russia. The agent, who spoke German, convinced Mennonite farmers—who had left their native Germany for Russia, hoping to find freedom there to practice their pacificist beliefs—to leave Russia and come to America. The Mennonites had been persecuted in Russia, too, for their beliefs. Therefore, in the ten years following the initial Mennonite migration in 1873, ten thousand Mennonites settled in Kansas.

The Mennonites, arriving with pieces of gold sewn into their clothing, were wealthier than most other emigrants to the West. But they also carried with them something far more precious than gold: bags of red winter wheat. With this winter wheat, the Mennonites were able to raise a cash crop and to prosper. They were the lucky ones.

Most new settlers were having a much harder time. The land they had been sold was anything but an Eden. The plains were dry and treeless. There was so little wood that the settlers had to use the surface layer of the land itself to construct their dwellings. These sod houses, as they were called, were held together by the tight weave of grass and roots that grew naturally in the topsoil.

The climate was not the temperate one described in the railroad pamphlets. Spring brought occasional floods that washed away small livestock and damaged homes of prairie sod. In summer, hot winds seared the plains as temperatures rose above 100° Farenheit. Frequent droughts parched the summer soil, and summer could also bring hordes of insects, such as grasshoppers. In 1874, a plague of grasshoppers ate all the crops (and just about everything else, including clothing!) from the Canadian border to northern Texas. In the fall, grasses were often so dry that thousands of acres went up in flames.

The worst season was the winter. Furious winds brought first dust, and later snow, along with temperatures below zero. Blizzards swept across the plains, even in the early spring. In 1872, a year in which 20,000 settlers had arrived in the Dakotas, a great blizzard began on Easter Sunday. The storm was so devastating that people froze to death between their kitchens and their chicken houses.

Worse for the settlers than the hardships, however, was the realization that the fertile land they had been promised was in fact hard, flat, and often resistant to the growing of crops. To whom could the new settlers go in their dismay? Most of the railroads had simply dumped the emigrants along the line, and showed no sympathy to their plight.

There were some rare exceptions: James J. Hill, the builder of the Northern Pacific, made genuine efforts to help the settlers along his line. His company had charged lower fees for land sections than the other railroads. Also, Hill had imported specially bred cattle that could be used for both beef and dairy herds, and provided this livestock without cost to settlers along his line. Most of the settlers, however, received no help. Many gave up and moved to the eastern states, or even farther west.

Those settlers who remained learned to survive by using new techniques. They dug deep wells to reach the water several hundred feet below the surface. They learned from the Mennonites methods for the cultivation of crops, such as wheat, that are resistant to drought. They tried new tools, such as the steel-tipped plows that cut through the dense roots of the prairie sod. They employed windmills to power pumps. By these means, and by perseverance and determination, the settlers gradually began to prosper.

In the early days, the railroads faced many difficulties which were ultimately overcome by rapidly developed technological innovations. Harsh winters were a problem for the railroads as they were for the pioneers.

The railroads were greatly useful to those settlers who stayed. The lines were used to transport supplies to the settlers and to ship their products to markets in the East. And the dreams of eastern manufacturers were ultimately fulfilled, for a large market for goods had been created amongst the settlers in the West.

Farmers were not the only newcomers the railroad brought to the West. Before the railroads, the cattle industry had developed slowly, but with the promise of a practical way to get beef to faraway markets, cattle ranchers saw great opportunities for prosperity. Although 5 million cattle had roamed the Southwest in 1860 (mostly in Texas), there were few buyers, though the population in the East had grown and the demand for meat had increased. The ranchers had no means to transport their valuable herds to the markets across the great expanses of open prairie. Cattle drives were long and costly, and often dangerous for the relatively few men to whom a huge herd was entrusted—one frightened steer could cause a deadly stampede.

The expansion of the railroads provided the long-range transportation that

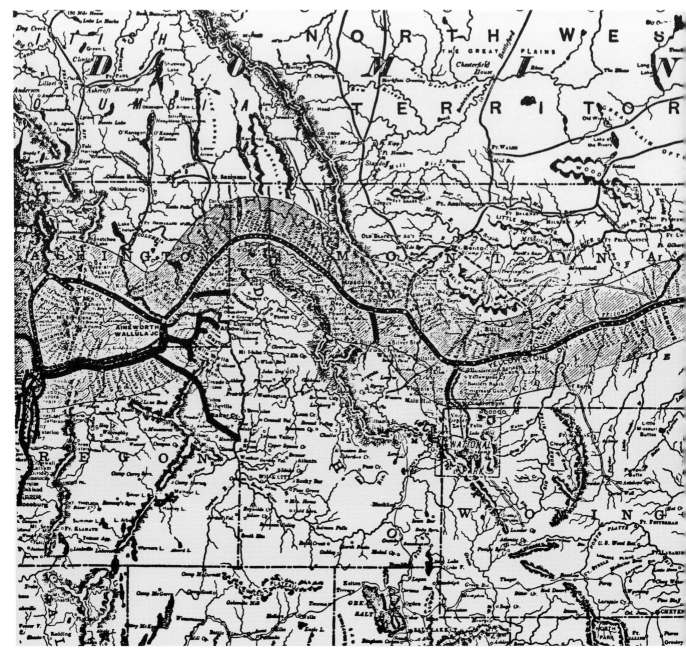

The Northern Pacific was the most successful transcontinental rail line.

made cattle ranching profitable. Cattlemen drove their vast herds much shorter distances, to new cattle centers along the railroad tracks. Cities like Abilene and Dodge City, both in Kansas, owed their existence to the cattle industry. In 1867, for example, Abilene consisted of twelve roofless huts. Three years later, thanks to the booming ranching industry, this cattle depot, with 300,000 head of livestock arriving annually for transportation east by rail, was a bustling business center.

The railroads' promise of a populous, prosperous West was fulfilled in another way, too. Western towns established before the building of the railroads often vied

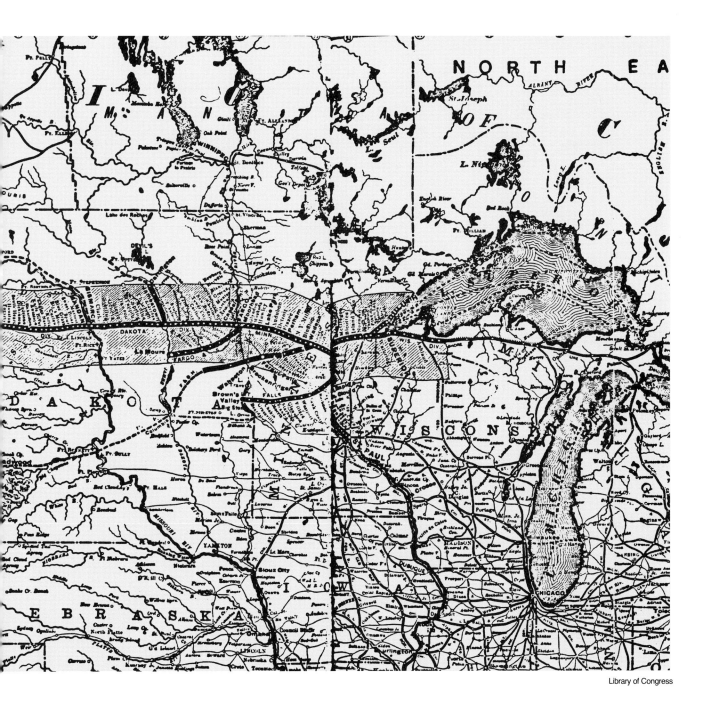

with each other to have the railroad pass nearby—residents of Salt Lake City, Utah, were furious that the Union Pacific would not be built close by. The townsfolk everywhere realized that the railroad would bring settlers, goods, and prosperity. In the Far West many towns were built alongside the railroad tracks. At the crossroads of two lines, towns often grew into cities. Los Angeles, for example, was built at the junction of the Santa Fe and the Southern Pacific lines.

The completion of the first transcontinental railroad had been the first step in changing forever the face of America, "from sea to shining sea."

AFTERWORD

ONE NATION, INDIVISIBLE

With the lands between the Mississippi and the West Coast, from the northern borders to the Rio Grande, settled by farmers and ranchers and peppered with towns large and small, America was finally truly a nation of "united states,"—linked by railway lines criss-crossing the land from the great cities of the East to the new growing urban centers of the West.

After the ceremony at Promontory Point, Bret Harte composed a poem to commemorate the event, entitled "What the Engines Said." It began:

What was it the engines said,
Pilots touching—head to head,
Facing on a single track,
Half a world behind each back?

Two halves of a continent had been linked that day at Promontory Point.

Certificate of Membership, Brotherhood of Railroad Firemen

Immigrants came from nations around the world to settle on the land the railroads had conquered and made accessible. Farmers and ranchers were able to speed their goods to cities and towns across the nation; manufacturers and craftspeople could distribute their goods to every settlement, large and small. And as more railroad routes were developed, the destinies of millions more Americans were linked in countless ways. The completion of the first transcontinental railroad line had ushered the country into an unparalleled period of growth and change.

Though the transcontinental railroad conceived by the idealistic Theodore Judah had been corrupted by the greed of stronger men, and though its construction had been fraught with perils and stained by prejudice and exploitation, it proved ultimately to have been the means by which this country grew to a new unity and a new prosperity, a turning point in the history of our nation.

INDEX

Page numbers in *italics* indicate illustrations.

SUGGESTED READING

BEEBE, LUCIUS. *The Central Pacific & the Southern Pacific Railroads.* Berkeley, Ca.: Howell-North, 1963.

BEST, GERALD M. *Iron Horses to Promontory.* San Marino, Ca.: Golden West Books, 1969.

GRISWOLD, WESLEY S. *A Work of Giants: Building the First Transcontinental Railroad.* New York: McGraw-Hill, 1962.

JENSEN, OLIVER. *The American Heritage History of Railroads in America.* New York: American Heritage Publishing Co. Inc., 1975.

TROTTMAN, NELSON S. *History of the Union Pacific.* Fairfield, N.J.:Kelley. Reprint of 1923 edition.

1 2 3 4 5 6 7 8 9 10—JDL—95 94 93 92 91 90 89 88 87 86